The American Way of Life

The Foreigners' Perspective

What you need to know

about living in the U.S.A

Claude Koehl

This Book is dedicated to:

- *everybody brave enough to move to an unfamiliar country*

- *Americans curious about foreigners' perspective of the U.S.A.*

- *all the clients I had the privilege to work with and*

- *last but not least, all the inspiring friends I have met on my own journey*

Index

Dear Reader

If you are reading this booklet, you either are about to visit or even relocate to the United States, have already arrived, or are simply curious about what aliens* could possibly find remarkable, unusual or even funny about America.

Most likely you already have some knowledge about the country's history, its economy, and its political system. You may even be familiar with its diverse communities and cultural components. But unless you've lived here for an extended period of time, some elements of the day-to-day living will surprise you.

With a touch of humor, this booklet turns a spotlight on things that are quintessentially American, as seen through the eyes of people from around the world. It will help newcomers realize that they are not alone in finding some customs funny or odd.

At the same time, the Foreigners' Perspective will give U.S. readers a better understanding about how their customs can be perceived by non-Americans, perhaps inspiring them to take a fresh look at their own cultural filter. After all, what is perceived as funny, strange or unusual is mainly a question of one's own unconscious bias and cultural perspective.

This book is a compilation of comments made by the numerous foreigners and expats I have worked with over the years. Of course, being an alien myself, I too had a lot to learn about my chosen domicile, and still at times, behave strangely from an American perspective.

I hope you will have fun reading this book.

Claude Koehl

* The word "alien" is a legal term that refers to any person who is not a citizen or national of the United States. It also refers to an extraterrestrial creature. You might want to ponder on that.

Dining and Food

The Foreigners' Perspective

Coffee

Foreign coffee lovers will tell you that the brew served in most U.S. restaurants, diners, and even private homes lacks the strength and flavor they are accustomed to.

Here's just one quick example. In the surprisingly ubiquitous coffee shops across the country there's often an option known as "Americano." That's when a good espresso is diluted with hot water. Enough said?

Despite the proliferation of espresso bars and coffee houses, drip-system filtered coffee is still a mainstay in public places and U.S. offices. Sitting on its hot plate, drip coffee starts the day way too weak then, as the hours wear on, strengthens until it turns into tar by late afternoon.

Foreigners with an affinity for rich coffee may find that strict avoidance of this type of brew is their best option. The very existence of drip coffee begs the question: Why is filtered coffee still so commonplace given there is no shortage of well-known coffee brands almost everywhere in the country? Looks like old habits die hard.

But don't worry. If you crave a good cup of coffee, ask any foreigner. They will knowingly nod and happily point you in the direction of a nearby coffeehouse where you are certain to find a coffee to your liking. And many do offer a dazzling selection of coffee varieties and concoctions.

By the way, grocery stores and specialty shops now carry a reasonably good selection of coffee beans for home brewing.

Cold Drinks

Order a soft drink, a glass of water, or any other cold drink and you're likely to receive a glass (or cup) filled to the brim with ice cubes, topped off by the beverage of your choice. Factually, only the space between the ice cubes will contain your drink.

By the way, this heavy-on-the-ice practice translates into healthy savings for the restaurant since ice cubes are definitively cheaper than any cocktails or carbonated drink

All that ice, of course, makes the drink super cold; to the point of giving you brain freeze if you drink it too fast. On the other hand, if you don't drink it fast enough, the melting cubes will dilute your beverage to tasteless swill. Damned if you do, damned if you don't.

To avoid the too-cold vs. too-watery dilemma, you will have to order your drink with a tag line: "Please only a few ice cubes" or even "Please no ice." It's not unlike the baffling quest to get a simple cup of black tea in Britain: "... and please no milk."

The good news on the cold-drink front, however, is the U.S. tradition of free refills. Especially in fast food or so-called "fast casual" eateries where once you place your order, you will have access to refills at no charge.

And water by the glass, of course with lots of ice, is always freely available in any restaurant.

Drink Sizes

Americans believe it healthy to have at least eight glasses of fluid a day (1.9 liters). Unfortunately, they tend to forget that since fluids are also absorbed through food, one does not need to actually drink that much.

Here the "you should drink liquids" admonition too frequently meets the American myth of "bigger is better." The result are beverage cups and bottle sizes of ginormous proportion. These include the Big Gulp, an aptly named trademark of the 7-Eleven convenience stores. The Big Gulp holds 30 ounces (0.89 liters), and it has even bigger siblings: the 44-ounce Super Big Gulp (1.3 liters) and the 53-ounce Extreme Big Gulp (1.57 liters).

By the way, there have been documented cases of athletes who became seriously sick (with hyponatremia) from drinking too much! More is definitively not always better.

Unfortunately, at 7-Eleven, as well as elsewhere, the oversized cups are generally not filled with water but with sugary drinks, thereby prompting some health advocates to lobby for legally banning these cup sizes.

Regrettably, the widespread practice of free and limitless refills, while a very nice customer perk, also encourages this unhealthy more-is-more approach to drinking. Another example of this practice is the so-called "bottomless coffee cup." In many restaurants, it is customary to keep topping-off your coffee cup at no additional charge.

Just imagine how jittery that will make you. And of course, it is a dubious benefit if you are among the expats who are less than thrilled by American coffee.

Ethnic Food

Long gone are the days when one had to search high and low for bread that was more than soft toast squares. The diversity of foods from around the world now available in the United States is truly remarkable. This variety is largely the result of generations of immigrants bringing their regional ingredients and cuisines to America.

With little effort, one can find almost any ethnic delicacy, from Peking roast duck Kaoya to French Vacherin cheese to Middle Eastern sweets like rosewater-flavored Lokum, if not directly in a store then through the internet.

In most cities, standard supermarkets now stock a variety of ethnic foods and ingredients mirroring their diverse local communities. This market segment is growing explosively.

Today, over 90 percent of Americans like to eat at least some ethnic foods, and 40 percent to 70 percent of U.S. consumers rate the availability of ethnic and cultural food as an important feature when choosing their primary supermarket (Statista 2014).

There are, of course, limits. Many Americans will still make a face when cow tongue, sticky rice cake, or even liver pâté is mentioned. The latter is interesting given that liverwurst, an all-time U.S. staple, is very much made of liver.

Fortunately, if you can entice your American friends to actually taste one of your regional specialties, they often will come around. After all, they are your friends...

Etiquette

You are probably aware that Americans have their own dining etiquette. For starters, once all the food on the plate has been cut, one is expected to switch the fork from the left hand to the right hand. (The left hand goes into rest mode, sitting on the tabletop or under the table on one's thigh.)

This basically means that the knife can no longer be used to help push food onto the fork. Obviously, this makes it difficult to get anything that cannot be speared onto the fork. And by the way, this protocol is correct even when eating spaghetti.

This custom might explain another widespread American eating habit. Many people here wield their fork "over-handed" in a childlike grip, presumably because it makes it easier to stab at the food. For non-Americans, it is odd seeing that practice employed by an adult.

Nevertheless, these dining habits might explain why Americans love eating at restaurants where they don't have to worry about cutlery, as the food served is destined to be eaten by hand. As one fast-food company slogan pledged, "If it doesn't get all over the place, it does not belong in your face."

On a different note, Americans do, of course, agree with the social convention of chewing only with a closed mouth. That said, particularly when chewing gum, too many seem comfortable talking and chomping at the same time. A bit shocking when it happens in a professional setting.

Fast Food

The sheer number of fast food restaurants and so-called "junk food" options in the United States is staggering.

The latest available data from 2015 shows the top 50 fast food chains alone had a collective 153,000-plus locations. They join the countless smaller mom-and-pop restaurants offering variations of fast food.

On average, Americans visit a fast food restaurant twice a week. However, the statistics also show that some Americans eat fast food three or more times a week, spending an average of $12.50 per meal. It is, therefore, not surprising that the competition among the various eateries is intense, and the variety of fast food restaurants (often offering a drive-thru option) keeps expanding. Together with the quickly growing segment of "fast casual restaurants" they account for more than 50% of sales in the entire restaurant sector.

At the same time, the assortment of ready-made junk food for home consumption (including for the microwave) is growing, and in all honesty, it is getting tastier.

Bottom line: Since junk food contains plenty of salt, fats, and sugars, it is not surprising that Americans are developing more and more of a taste for foods that combine sweet and savory. An additional gooey consistency also seems to be a big plus.

Since one cannot ignore (or understate) the convenience of U.S. fast food, it is heartening to know that as the menus of junk food chains evolve, more healthy options become available even at traditional fast food chains.

Noise

Many foreigners remark upon the noise levels in public places. Restaurants are no exception.

A 2016 Zagat Survey found that, on average, the sound level in U.S. restaurants easily reaches up to 80 decibels. That is as loud as a grinding garbage disposal or a freight train passing nearby! Some restaurant critics cite noise as their chief complaint and have begun noting an eatery's decibel level as part of their review.

Several factors contribute to this noisiness. Coffeehouses, bars, and restaurants all tend to play music rather loudly while the buildings are often poorly soundproofed. (Some play music and have the television on.) Additionally, while restaurant patrons in many countries tend to speak in hushed tones to keep their conversation private, U.S. customers often behave as they would if at home, paying little attention to whether others can hear them.

Together these factors create a vicious cycle. As the loud music amps up the noise, patrons automatically tend to speak louder to make themselves heard. Question: Why does no one connect cause and effect and turn the music down? This is an especially pertinent question given that the loudness of restaurants has now become the top complaint of Americans themselves.

Smart entrepreneurs have started tapping this as an opportunity: There are now apps on the market that allow patrons to measure and tag the noise level of an establishment.

Organic Food

Organic food is one of the fastest-growing segments of American agriculture, according to a 2016 U.S. Department of Agriculture (USDA) report. In the last few years, the variety of healthy or organic food choices available at stores, restaurants, and even fast-food joints across the country has risen dramatically.

Although the Centers for Disease Control and Prevention finds that fast food still accounts for about 10 percent of the daily calories of the average American, the food options across the country have undoubtedly become healthier and more varied in recent decades.

No matter where you live in the United States today, you now should be able to find organic food at nearby stores and restaurants. Lately, a substantial selection of organic products has gone mainstream, putting them in nearly three-quarters of conventional grocery stores (USDA 2017).

And, if you can't find an organic product you want in a store near you, there is always the online option. You can order organic products over the internet and have them shipped to your door—from organic grass-fed beef to Community-Supported Agriculture (CSA) subscription services. Farmers' markets featuring organic foods have also become a wonderful fixture in many U.S. cities.

Products catering to people following other diet restrictions and preferences, among them high-protein, low-carb, vegan, or gluten-free, are now widely available in urban areas, and are becoming easier to find in even smaller towns.

The Foreigners' Perspective

Portion Sizes

It is an open secret that food portions in America are humongous. (The sometimes exception is food served in upscale restaurants).

There is an actual competition among restaurants to see who can serve the biggest burger (7 pounds/3 kg), the biggest pizza (4.5 ft2/0.4 m2), the biggest and juiciest steak (28 ounces/0.8 kg).

One must wonder, how these places test their claim about serving the "world's" biggest, tastiest, or juiciest something.

Restaurants offering these supersized deals often attract customers by promising a free meal if the customer can eat the oversized menu item within a prescribed time limit, such as 30 minutes.

Gorging down an overly abundant meal may not be an attractive proposition for everybody. But there are still plenty of people willing to attempt such a crazy feat for a free meal and the potential honor of having their name immortalized on the restaurant's "Wall of Champions".

Still, let's not forget that there is another aspect to large portions. They allow the customer to pay once and eat twice (or sometimes even three times).

In the United States, if anything is left on your plate at a restaurant, the wait staff will ask if you'd like a box to take the leftovers home. And there's no longer a need to pretend it is a "doggie bag" for a pet waiting at home. In fact, restaurants have completely stopped using that term.

Processed Food

The selection of processed foods in supermarkets across the nation is mind blowing. If the statistics are to be believed, processed foods make up to 70 percent of the average U.S. diet. Here are some iconic (and unhealthy) examples.

- Admittedly, spreading soft cheese on a cracker can be challenging, as the crackers usually break into pieces. Say "hello" to an alternative: cheese in a can! Gone is the cracked-cracker problem. As for taste, you'll have to be the judge of that.

- Another product favored by a majority of Americans comes in a can. Instead of heating butter or liquid oils to grease a pan, a cooking spray is used. This spray consists of some form of oil, an emulsifier, and a propellant like propane. Perhaps no further comment is needed?

- An all-time favorite, chicken nuggets, can be found in store freezer sections. (U.S. youngsters live on these.) The morsels, which come already breaded and deep fried, consist largely of fats, cartilage, blood vessels, nerves, preservatives and stabilizers—not, as one might assume, primarily of muscle meat. Feel free to do your own tasting if you dare.

- Spam is another iconic processed food product. This salty canned meat has the texture of a meat-jelly-sponge and consists mainly of fat and preservatives. It had its heyday during World War II.

And in case you are wondering, junk email is called spam because of a Monty Python sketch about the product.

Seating

At the entrances of U.S. restaurants, there is often a sign stating: "Please wait to be seated." In other words, here you are not supposed to simply walk in and sit down. Instead, you are expected to wait for the hostess to assign you a table. In case you are wondering, indeed this is a position mostly filled by women.

When restaurants are busy, and many reservations must be honored, the need for organizing the seating order is understandable. But when the restaurant is half empty, the wait seems unnecessary (especially considering how well self-seating works in other cultures). Fact is, the hostess will often stop you from simply seating yourself.

On the other hand, while seating may take some time, getting the bill delivered does not. To avoid having your plate being whisked away while still enjoying your meal, it is recommended to never set your cutlery down. Once you stop eating, waiters are trained to clear your plate and your cutlery even if other members of your party are still enjoying their meal.

No doubt, it is nice not to have to sit in front of dirty plates for an extended period of time and to have the bill (generally called "the check") presented in a timely fashion. But for foreigners, this very expeditious and well-oiled process might at times feel like being thrown out of the restaurant.

Obviously, in the United States "time is money" and restaurants count on turning over the tables in their establishment multiple times per evening. The focus here is more on filling one's belly than on the social aspect of the meal.

Service

Without any doubt, the customer is at the heart of the hospitality industry everywhere. But what is considered good customer service is largely determined by culture.

Old-world service standards for instance require waiters to be attentive but low-profile. In the United States, by contrast, wait staff are expected to be much more personable and engaging.

This begins when the waiter introduces him or herself by first name and starts a friendly chat with you and the guests in your party. In some ways, it is rather charming. And it is definitely more uplifting than the grumpy service you get all too often in Europe.

However, if you are used to old-world standards, or even the largely discreet Asian approach to service, it can feel rather intrusive. After all, you are at the restaurant to meet with your friends and not to get to know the waiter.

The root of this personalized customer service model may be less about the egalitarian way of life in the United States as it is about the fact that restaurant workers earn very low wages. Waiters strongly rely on tips to make a halfway decent living. Under these circumstances, it makes a lot of sense to be outgoing and friendly, to actively establish a personal connection with each guest.

Don't be surprised if you are greeted by your first name next time you visit the same restaurant.

Selection & Waste

Supermarkets are the perfect illustration of the Land of Plenty. As mentioned before, their selection of foods is simply flabbergasting. Even within the same product category, there are many brands and options to choose from. It is more than tempting to try everything at least once and to fill the shopping cart with items you would not normally eat.

Additionally, there are also membership-driven wholesale stores dominated by "family sized" products that seem geared toward households of six or more (even though the average family size is 3.1 people).

Not surprisingly, up to 40 percent of the food is ultimately thrown away even though almost 70 percent of it is potentially still edible. In 2018 the Natural Resources Defense Council put the value of this discarded food at $218 billion a year, adding that it also generates harmful greenhouse gases as it decomposes in landfills.

The message here is that even if you now own one of those huge U.S. refrigerators, don't get too tempted by the vast selection at the grocery stores. Of course, it can't hurt to try some of the products at least once. Still, you might potentially want to hold on to your own cultural habits of shopping for fresh, local produce several times a week.

If you do succumb to the bounty, be aware that today there are apps designed to help tackle food waste. Sharing your surplus food could make a huge difference as sadly about 12 percent of the U.S. population goes hungry too often.

BBQ SAUCE

SUGAR

Sugar & Sweets

Did you know that a typical 20-ounce (0.6 liters) bottle of sugar-sweetened soda contains the equivalent of 15 to 18 sugar cubes?

And savory processed foods contain lots of sugar too. For instance, just two (2) tablespoons of a typical American barbecue sauce may carry as much as 12 grams of sugar (about three cubes).

If statistics are to be believed, the average American still gets about 16 percent of her or his daily calories from sugars added to food and beverages during their production. That's more than 50 percent above what is recommended by the U.S. Food and Drug Administration, the country's reference institution in these matters. Obviously, if savory foods contain that much sugar, desserts, confections, and candies can be expected to be even sweeter.

Indeed, U.S. pastries take sweet to the next level. Not only are they generally overly sweet, but they are also excessively fatty, as they are often covered in thick blankets of buttercream frosting, such as is the case with the iconic cupcake. (For your information, one single chocolate cupcake with frosting can easily contain up to 500 calories.)

Of course, other world regions, including the Middle East, create similarly sweet desserts but there the portion sizes are generally much smaller.

The sweetness level of U.S. food may take some time getting used to. Alternatively, you can always learn how to bake your own pastry if you don't know how to yet.

Tipping

In some countries, you might have to remind your server that you've already asked more than once for the bill. In the United States, you will be presented with the check almost before you have finished your meal.

You will quickly learn that the bill received does not actually contain your final tally. In fact, you are expected to calculate and add in a tip in order to arrive at the total cost of your meal.

The customary rate for tipping is 15 percent to 25 percent of the food bill (not counting the tax), or a little more or less depending on how satisfied you are with the service received.

Lately, many restaurants will help you with the math by adding a line at the bottom of your check indicating how much 15, 20, or 25 percent of your bill represents. Be aware that if you are dining with a large group, an 18 percent gratuity will automatically be tacked onto the bill.

From a foreigner's point of view, this does not seem logical as most groups tend to order more dishes. From a U.S. perspective, however, it makes total sense. A larger group tends to linger longer at the table, which in turn means less turnover per table and ultimately less income and tips.

For your information, even with an 18 percent gratuity already included, many Americans will top it up to 25% or more. And by the way, many Americans do consider it extremely bad-mannered not to leave a generous tip, to the point of sometimes making up the difference for you.

Home Sweet Home

Bathrooms & Toilets

Sorry, but we must indeed talk about toilets. Alas, they can be a source of irritation for visitors and expats.

Obviously, the basic goal of toilets anywhere is the same, and the different systems across the planet all achieve their objective. But the models and techniques used to accomplish this goal span a wide spectrum, from the squat toilets of China to the hands-free Japanese toilet-bidet (with heated seats and a dryer function).

Additionally, different cultures rely on differing flushing systems to elicit the desired result. The methods range from gravity to suction flushing. In each case the amount of water used, the swirl created, as well as the noise level can vary considerably.

It is amazing how a task that normally is completed unconsciously can suddenly become the focus of one's attention when using an unfamiliar system. Depending on your country of origin, it might take a bit of time to get used to the rather swirly and frequently noisy U.S. flushing systems.

Rest assured, you are in good company if you find yourself uneasily surveilling the flushing function during the first few months after your arrival.

The good news in all this is that while many countries have only one toilet per apartment or even per house, in the United States the toilet standard is closer to one bathroom for almost every bedroom.

Home Sweet Home

The Foreigners' Perspective

Bedrooms

The central element of any bedroom is obviously the bed. The U.S. bed dimensions—full, queen, king—are quite close to the metric bed sizes available around the world. The standard mattress widths are almost a match, while U.S. beds tend to be proportionally a bit longer. But the bedding, like blankets and pillows, definitively tends to be oversized in comparison.

American beds usually comprise three parts: a bed frame, a (coil) mattress, and a box spring. (If mattress commercials are anything to go by, the higher the coil count, the better the bed.) Together, these three elements create a bed that is considerably higher than in most other parts of the world. The box spring alone can add as much as 9 inches (23 cm) to the overall height.

In other words, while for instance, in Japan the tatamis are at floor level, with an American bed you barely need to bend your knees to get in and out.

Beyond the bed, the gold standard for any master bedroom in the United States is direct access to a dedicated, private bathroom. Additional bedrooms often also have dedicated bathrooms, although they might not always have direct access (or be en-suite, as connected bathrooms are called).

This bedroom-bathroom duo is particularly valued by people who do not like to share their bathroom, or who are particularly privacy conscious, and can afford this luxury. You might easily come to appreciate this standard, if you are sharing your home with a guest or a roommate.

Home Sweet Home

The Foreigners' Perspective

Ceiling Fans

Simply by having watched American films and by being an attentive observer, you might have noticed the many ceiling fans. They are frequently installed in every room of the house. Often, they double as light fixtures.

There is no doubt that ventilators can keep us more comfortable on a hot day or night. However, to foreigners, it is surprising how widespread they are, even in parts of the United States where temperatures rarely exceed 30° C (86° Fahrenheit).

And don't think for a minute that having a ceiling fan in each room means that the home does not also have a central air conditioning system.

The available selection of ceiling fans (just like the food choices in the grocery store) is immense. A quick online search of do-it-yourself stores (better known as DIYs) reveals more than 1,800 ceiling fan options, with styles ranging from bohemian to farmhouse to industrial, with or without a light fixture included.

The price range is equally broad in scope, with basic ceiling fans starting as low as $30 while fancier ones cost over $4,000. Still, even the most expensive fans are obviously more economical to run than any air conditioning system.

But make no mistake, many Americans will run ceiling fans and air conditioners concurrently, which is definitively neither economical nor ecological.

Countertops

Kitchens are the true heart of any home, and countertops seem to be the heart of any U.S. kitchen. There are essentially two main types of countertops in the majority of American residences: tile and natural-stone.

Tile is found mainly in lower-end properties as the surface will always be slightly uneven and the grout between the tiles stains easily and therefore is hard to keep clean.

Natural-stone countertops, meanwhile, are certainly more durable and sanitary but they are also very pricey and need yearly maintenance. Still, natural stone countertops have become an obsession, according to U.S. news website Vox. And that claim can easily be confirmed by anyone watching one of the many popular home remodeling shows on TV.

Why do Americans prefer natural-stone countertops when so many other solid-surfaces (e.g. acrylic, polyester, engineered stone) of comparable quality, needing less maintenance are available at better prices? Maybe quartz, granite and marble have come to signify durability, timelessness and high-class finish in a rapidly changing U.S. society where those qualities can seem elusive?

If at some point you opt for home ownership in the United States and consider any kitchen remodeling, your best strategy is to watch a home remodeling show to learn about current trends. Efficiency, maintenance and personal preferences aside, your decision could make a big difference in how well your property will sell once you put it on the market.

Doorknobs

Typically U.S. hardware stores and do it yourself stores (DIYs) are all very well stocked. A quick online search of major hardware stores brought up more than 4,000 doorknob styles.

But of those, only about 1,300 were actual door handles, which are what is most common in many other countries. For reasons unknown, round doorknobs are clearly favored in the United States. They are particularly widespread in residential real estate as you can easily observe for yourself.

Now, there is nothing wrong with round doorknobs, provided you have at least one free and dry hand. Because if not, good luck with getting the door open. A door handle, on the other hand (so to speak), can easily be depressed with almost any body part, even an elbow or a foot. It is perfectly serviceable even when your hands are full (or wet).

By the way, something else to watch for is the placement of the round doorknobs. Sometimes they are installed so close to the edge of the door that one has to be careful not to catch a hand in the doorframe as the door swings open. (Wedge your hand just once between the door and the frame and you will forever be wary of these doorknobs.)

All this said, for pet owners, there is one very considerable advantage to round doorknobs; They make it hard, if not impossible, for your pets to open doors on their own. That must count for something.

Home Sweet Home

The Foreigners' Perspective

Doors

America is a safety conscious country. It is, therefore, interesting that doors are chosen more for their decorative properties than their security features.

A quick online search will turn up a huge selection of over 4,000 front doors and around 3,000 interior doors. But for some reason many front doors, especially the fancier ones, showcase some kind of glass window pane.

It is wonderful how these panes allow natural light to enter a foyer or hallway, yet it seems paradoxical to equip a front door with glass (most of the not-shatter-proof kind). After all, Americans are so concerned with security that many install alarm systems to protect their homes. Doesn't a glass pane on the front door weaken privacy and safety barriers?

And what about the interior doors? Here too, Americans seem to favor doors with panels made of wood or glass. Though in Craftsman-style houses, the interior doors will often have louvers instead of panes.

Either way, none of these options create effective barriers to noise or dust since interior doors in residential homes are rarely installed perfectly flush with the door frames.

The decorative, rather than functional elements that dominate U.S. door styles, reveal a fondness for an old-fashioned, "traditional" look that surprisingly can also be found in other aspects of American life (e.g. furniture, architecture, print design).

Electricity

Around the world, domestic appliances are built to run on either 110 or 220 (230) volts, depending on each country's standard. In North America, that official standard in households is 110 volts (while the nominal power is 120 volts).

Unsurprisingly, there is a specific standard for the corresponding electrical plugs. Even if you already know this, you might still be surprised by how these U.S. plugs are constructed.

For one thing, plugs are directional (polarized) with one prong wider than the other, so there is only one way to insert a plug into an outlet. Newer household appliances still often come equipped solely with this bipolar plug and not with a grounded tri-pronged plug. Furthermore, these prongs are flimsy and can be easily bent. If you are not careful, this can happen even while simply unplugging an appliance. (Being pliable, at least they can effortlessly be bent back into shape.)

Depending on your own cultural background, the electrical outlets might also seem a bit rickety. And, again, unless you live in a newer home, they might not be set up to accommodate any tri-pronged appliances.

A word of warning: Even with the lower 110 voltage standard in America, do-it-yourself electrical repairs or installations are not recommended unless you really know what you are doing.

Remember: The risk is primarily the electrical charge and not the voltage.

Faucets

Once upon a time, water faucets had two separate handles, one for hot water and one for cold water.

Today, there are very many single-handle faucets available for easy, one-handed mixing of hot and cold water. Given that, it is curious that so many old-style faucets are found in bathrooms and kitchens across the United States. A random online search brings up about 20,000 different faucet handle models; fully two-thirds are two-handed.

For reasons unknown, one model, the so-called clear, non-metallic faucet, is particularly popular. With this two-handled faucet, both hands must be used to achieve the desired water temperature as otherwise the mixing will take forever. A difficult challenge arises when you try to readjust the temperature of these faucets with soapy hands. It is very difficult to get a proper grip on the sleek plastic surface.

Additionally, once you are ready to rinse, the equally popular standard short spout will leave little room to get the soap off your hands.

Here comes the worst part. Should you have to scrub this type of handle, you will come to realize that its countless planes and slants makes the cleaning another almost impossible task.

Even knowing that this faucet is the absolute cheapest one available, it is hard to understand how it ever could became so popular. It is not even good looking.

Heating & Cooling

An estimated 90 percent of residential houses in the United States have forced air heating and cooling systems. The obvious advantage of this type of system is the short time it takes to reach the set temperature and the fact that the same ductwork and vents can be used for both heating and cooling the home.

The main disadvantages are the strong air flow and the stratified temperature differences that result in a room. Nor is such a system especially energy efficient: There is a lot of temperature loss while the air is forced through the (mostly uninsulated) ductwork. And, without regular filter changes, the air in these systems may carry allergens like dust and mold.

But that is not all. Do you remember learning at school about warm air rising? Scientifically more correct: Air, like any other gas, expands when heated, making it less dense than when it is cold. Since warm air obviously floats on top of cold air, it makes little sense to position air vents at the top of the walls or even directly in the ceiling.

How is the hot air blown through these vents supposed to ever reach your feet?

By the way, since a simple motor forces the air through the vents, this type of heating and cooling system also tends to be rather noisy. Luckily for them, most Americans are unbothered by noise.

Garbage Disposal

Most North American kitchens come with the following standard equipment: refrigerator, oven, microwave, and, unlike their counterparts in many other countries, a waste/garbage disposal.

Composting is the eco-friendliest solution for getting rid of perishable foods, but it is not an option available (or of interest) to everybody. Garbage disposals can seriously help reduce the amount of food sent to landfills and keep your home more sanitary, as less garbage will sit for an extended time in the trash can. Grinding and flushing perishable food in a disposal can also reduce garbage transport costs and gas buildup.

It is, therefore, helpful to know how to use this standard kitchen amenity:

- Small amounts of table scraps can go into the disposal, but cold water needs to be running while the food scraps are being ground.

- Stringy and fibrous vegetables, eggshells, and starchy foods should never be put down the disposal. (And no coffee grounds either.)

- Pouring grease down the drain is a no-no as it will film over the grinders' teeth.

- Avoid dropping cutlery or anything else metallic into the garbage disposal, and never reach into a running garbage disposal!

Garbage disposals can be helpful and efficient if used as intended. However, if you can't get used to them, simply cover the sinkhole with one of the strainers available at any supermarket for a few dollars.

Home Sweet Home

The Foreigners' Perspective

Microwave Ovens

The convenience of microwave ovens is undeniable. Around the world, this technology has won over consumers. U.S. homes usually come equipped with a microwave oven as many Americans barely (know how to) use their conventional oven or stovetop and only about 10 percent actually like to cook.

The number and range of processed microwavable products at supermarkets are impressive and, against all odds, some are surprisingly good. The convenience of microwave popcorn is hard to beat. And some organic foods cook well in the microwave, sometimes even better than on the stovetop.

What differentiates microwaves in the United States is their placement in the kitchen. They are commonly installed over the range/stove as an integral part of the cabinetry. And they are ordinarily combined with an air-fan for the stove below.

Because of this, one must be mindful about choosing the right-sized replacement appliance if the microwave breaks down. The dimensions of the available opening will determine your options. Call on a professional for the installation—unless you are very confident in your handyman skills.

By the way, corn on the cob, a summer staple in the United States, cooks both quickly and perfectly well in the microwave. There are many recipes available online, but this works every time: wrap the ears of corn in moist paper towels, put them on a microwave-safe dish, and microwave for about five minutes. Yummy!

The Foreigners' Perspective

Refrigerators

If you are a fan of American movies you might already be aware that side-by-side refrigerators/freezers are the standard in the United States. This preference, once again echoes the U.S. "bigger is better" mantra.

A typical version of the appliance measures between 22.5 and 30 cubic feet (0.64-0.85 m^2)!

These refrigerators would be way too large for a great many kitchens around the world. In Japan and Europe, the refrigerator and freezer capacity commonly are barely a third of the American volume, measuring about 8 to 11 cubic feet (0.23-0.31 m^2).

Huge fridges, of course, accommodate the U.S. habit of shopping for groceries only once a week or even less frequently. Question: Which came first, the mammoth fridges or the weekly shopping habits?

Currently, most of these gigantic refrigerators come with an ice-maker and water dispenser built right into the door exterior. In other words, you can fill a glass with ice cubes and top it off with cold water without even opening the refrigerator door. For this technical feat, the refrigerators are connected directly to a waterline and have a built-in filtering system allowing them to produce clean water and ice cubes.

People from outside the United States are often dumbfounded when they see the size of these monstrous appliances for the first time. Standing before the appliance they will comment at length on its functionalities and mammoth size. Now, that is rather funny from an American perspective.

The Foreigners' Perspective

Television

In many U.S. households, the television is on almost as long as someone is home and awake. (Sadly, sometimes even beyond that.) In these homes, the arrival of guests does not necessarily mean the TV will be turned off or that the sound will be muted.

Unfortunately, much of the programming consists of "reality" TV shows built on premises, such as who is the best talent in a specific field (e.g., song, dance, cooking). Additionally, a considerable number of these shows are aired repeatedly, sometimes even re-airing twice in the same week.

What is truly surprising about U.S. television is the sheer number of talk shows, political or otherwise. Americans most definitively have the gift of gab and while talking about politics or religion may be off limits in social settings, that is not the case on TV.

For many years, the air time spent on content versus on commercials has been inching towards a 50:50 split. Only lately have media companies started to slash the number of commercials on cable channels because of the emergence of streaming services.

Still, the same ads are often run more than once within an hour of programming. Does it truly make them more more memorable or just more annoying?

The order in which the ads air can be entertaining in itself. An ad for fat, gooey, calorie-laden food is often followed by an ad for pills to counter heartburn. What does that tell you?

Home Sweet Home

The Foreigners' Perspective

Windows | Screens

In 1873, the first window screens were installed in U.S. homes to keep flies and mosquitos at bay, with the promise of making a difference "between absolute misery and sweetest comfort," according to the National Museum of American History.

Since then, screens have become so popular that they now represent another American gold standard. Here window screens are truly an integral part of any new window installation. Screens are fitted to each window size and can easily be taken out to be cleaned or, if necessary, to be replaced.

Even for older homes with windows of unusual sizes, there are plenty of kits on the market for do-it-yourself solutions. Alternatively, online stores will deliver custom-made window screens right to your doorstep.

And if you know yourself to be a favorite target of hungry mosquitoes but do love to sleep with your windows open, you will definitively come to appreciate window screens.

They are a much more comfortable solution than dousing yourself in sticky and stinky bug repellent. And because of the prevalence of window screens everywhere, you will not even have to worry if you are planning to stay overnight at a friend's house.

Once you realize how easy they are to install, and how affordable window screens can be, you will be left pondering why they are not standard in all the countries where mosquitos are a real plague.

Home Sweet Home

The Foreigners' Perspective

Windows | Treatments

Exterior shutters are not common in America, although rolling exterior window shutters, for example, offer optimal security and privacy.

You may spot exterior shutters in some colder regions of the country where, as in many northern European countries, they are valued for the additional protection they provide from high winds and snow storms. And some larger stately homes on the East Coast may be equipped with folding exterior shutters, but even those are not typical.

Considering the extreme weather in many parts of the United States, it would make a lot of sense to invest more in exterior window treatments.

As for inside the house, the range of window treatments available in stores and online is once again huge, and you should be able to easily find products to your liking or similar to the ones from back home.

Based on the range of products available as well as personal observations, it appears that blinds and shades are more popular in America than curtains and draperies. This may be explained by price and ease of installation.

By the way, in cases where homeowners do invest in curtains or drapes, they often go all out and color-coordinate them with the wall paint, the furniture, and even the throw cushions.

For your information: Blinds and shades are usually considered an integral part of the residence and, as such, transfer to the new owner when a home is sold.

Windows | Types

One last thing about windows that might surprise you. Sliding windows are more or less the norm in the United States.

To open these windows, one needs to either slide:

- the bottom window pane vertically up or
- the side window pane horizontally to the right or left

In either case, only one pane of the window moves, while the other half remains fixed. In other words, the visible window size is bigger than the window opening, and airflow is limited to the opening of the sliding window pane.

This is a limitation that, for instance, Europe's hinged tilt-and-turn windows do not have. There are most certainly historical reasons for this cultural preference, but it can be frustrating if you are accustomed to throwing windows wide open.

In older homes the restricted window openings might not be your only source of irritation as over the years the mostly wooden windows have been painted and re-painted, to the point where they are difficult to open and close.

You may also be surprised to see that by far not all windows are double glazed. That might be of little importance in warmer regions of the country, but it can make a big difference in colder regions.

But don't worry. This being the United States, for the right price you can have any type of window imaginable installed—and have the work done quickly.

On The Road Again

The Foreigners' Perspective

Cars

Small cars with a suspension tuned for small winding roads, which are the norm in many parts of the world, are not the first choice of American drivers. They clearly prefer the comfort of a soft suspension made for cruising on long highways with barely a turn in sight.

Generally, all cars built for this market, and not just American car brands, are fitted with a relatively soft suspension.

In their hearts, Americans still love big cars, and, particularly, big trucks with souped-up suspensions that would not be considered legal in many other countries.

Odds are that you will be caught off guard by the number of pimped-up cars and customized trucks you will encounter. And at street fairs, be prepared to admire classic low-rider cars with hydraulic suspensions that will leave you speechless. Lastly, in rural areas, watch out for monster trucks. Their wheels can be almost as tall as you are.

That said, car-crazy America is undergoing a shift. Today, many more vehicle owners are interested in fuel efficiency and keeping their transportation costs down. There is also a whole new "Tesla generation" of electric and hybrid cars spotted more frequently on the roadways.

Bottom line: Although the legal speed limit in the United States might be lower than in some other countries, there are many things that U.S. car aficionados do with their vehicles that would not be permitted elsewhere in the world.

Drive-thru & Drive-in

Drive-thrus are a truly American invention, pioneered in the 1930s. As the name implies, a drive-thru allows drivers to stay in their cars while getting served. The notion behind the practice is that it will save you time, although that is definitively not the case when drive-through lines are long. The following services are available in most states:

- Ordering of food and beverages

- Refilling medical prescriptions at pharmacies

- Withdrawing money from bank accounts

- Getting married

- Dropping off mail

There are even drive-thru mortuaries, where motorists can take part in viewings of the recently deceased by driving by a window where the coffin is displayed.

Drive-ins, on the other hand, are no longer as popular as they were in the 1950s and 60s. They feature big parking lots where drivers park in marked zones before service personnel take their orders either via stationary microphones or by coming to the driver's car window. The food is then delivered directly to the car, sometimes by servers on roller-skates. How fun is that?

The open-air drive-in movie theater, another uniquely American experience, is not to be missed, even if you are no longer a teenager (interested in making out in the back seat). The challenge is finding a drive-in movie, as currently there are just about 300 operating across the country, down from a peak of 4,000 in the late 1950s.

Toot One's Horn

The United States is by no means a quiet culture. Sounds and noises are a constant, from background music in stores and restaurants to cheerleaders encouraging their teams at top of their lungs at sporting events.

Modern-day built-in auditory notifications are also integral components of any motor vehicle. Among the noise-makers are warnings that beep when you back up and alarms that sound if a seat belt is not buckled or a door is not shut tight.

Quite many Americans enjoy making their cars even noisier, by changing out the exhaust pipe, pumping up the car's audio system, or boosting the engine sound. And drivers of muscle cars or of the iconic American motorcycle, Harley Davidson, might even argue that they have an obligation to make their vehicle sound as loud as possible. Heck, a true aficionado will brave the law in good conscience and go for more.

What is therefore truly surprising, is how little Americans use their car horn, while in some countries, drivers seem to believe that laying on the horn will magically help improve the traffic flow.

Not so in the United States. The most you might hear is a quick tooting. Should a driver actually hit the horn, chances are he or she is a foreigner who has not yet adapted to the American way.

There are some notable exceptions. Miami and of course New York are, for instance, horn-honking towns.

Transmission

Cars are still a central element of U.S. life. Unless you live in one of the bigger cities with good public transit, getting around without a car remains a challenge.

Car ownership is still on the rise and that means more highway congestion, including the dreaded on-the-road stress that comes with rush hour.

Not least because of the stop-and-go of their daily commute, most Americans prefer cars with an automatic transmission, even if they do not offer quite the same level of control as a stick-shift. (Automatic transmissions are definitively easier to drive in rush hour.)

Since most U.S. vehicles have bigger engines (e.g. engine displacement above two liters/122 cubic inches) than, say, in Europe, the type of transmission has little impact on the car's overall power anyhow. Only lately, have sales of smaller cars, in some parts of the country, increased.

By the way, most Americans never learn how to drive a car with a stick shift. This in turn can be quite a handicap when renting a car abroad. (And yes, many don't have much experience with parallel parking either and try to avoid it as much as possible.)

To improve the resale value of your car, it is recommended that you buy a car with an automatic transmission (even if you personally prefer a stick shift). This will also be very helpful if you ever end up in a situation where somebody else needs to drive your car.

The Foreigners' Perspective

Tailgate Parties

Have you ever attended a baseball or football game, or even a concert in the United States? If so, you may already be familiar with "tailgating." Tailgate parties in the parking lot are an essential part of the event experience.

When tailgate parties started, people simply congregated around a truck's open tailgate for a beer and a bite to eat. Today tailgate parties have evolved into elaborate rituals. There now exists a full range of tailgate party supplies, from special barbecue grills (with built-in coolers) to tents used to stake out space for the tailgate party.

No longer is a cooler of beer and some potato chips enough. Trucks are now filled to the brim with all kinds of food, beverages and supplies. A tailgate party is a unique U.S. tradition that everybody should experience at least once.

If you do participate in a tailgate party, you should remember that many of the participating car owners are very proud of their shiny, often souped-up vehicles. (Also keep in mind that these are definitively not teetotaler gatherings.)

You will do well to avoid behavior that could potentially be interpreted as disrespectful. For instance, do not lean against somebody else's car, get into an argument about anything, or cheer for the guest team in the wrong parking lot section.

Just enjoy the crazy party!

Traffic Flow

We are all familiar with images of U.S. highways innumerable lanes, cloverleaf interchanges, and traffic jams. What is less known is the actual architecture of highway entrances and exits, how traffic flows here are engineered, and why they so easily spark traffic jams.

On cloverleaf ramps, cars coming onto a highway, as well as those exiting it, literally cross each other's paths. Cars merging the highway need to accelerate, while those exiting need to slow down. The design of these ramps, as well as the unpopularity of so-called "zipper merging," inevitably leads to daily traffic jams! The entering or exiting on a cloverleaf ramp is truly a terrifying experience for many foreigners, as one must act very quickly and decidedly to cross lanes.

Some states recently launched campaigns to teach drivers to take turns when merging and exiting highways in the hope this will improve traffic flow and prevent some accidents. Still, be prepared to proceed with caution.

One system that does indeed help traffic flow and should be replicated in other countries are the carpool lanes. Those are highway lanes solely dedicated for use by cars carrying two or more people. Alas, at some point, even these drivers must reintegrate with the general lanes to exit the highway. At rush hour, that's the point when another traffic jam is born.

A word of warning: Proper use of carpool lanes is enforced strictly and the penalty for violations can be very costly.

Traffic Lights

Most foreigners are positively surprised to learn about the nearly nationwide law allowing right-hand turns on red lights. (The United States is among only a handful of countries—including Canada, China, and Saudi Arabia—that permits this.)

Some states also allow left turns onto one-way streets when the light is red, but the driver must come to a full stop first. Either way, once foreigners experience for themselves how turning on red keeps traffic moving better, they embrace it eagerly.

While turns on red are fairly easy to adopt, other things about U.S. traffic lights are more difficult to get used to:

- Placement
  U.S. traffic lights are positioned on the other side of the crossing. In many other regions (e.g. Japan and Europe), they are on the same side of the intersection as the drivers even though that can make it hard to have a good view of the lights.

- Length of traffic light phases
  Everybody appreciates a long green light, but nobody likes to wait at a red light. Some of the lengthier red-light phases here will have many Europeans grumbling about the extended wait time.

Interestingly, if you are daydreaming while waiting for a red-light to finally change to green, most drivers behind you will wait patiently for you to wake up. Very rarely will the honk at you. After all, queuing is a way of life in America.

SLOW OR STOP

LEFT TURN

RIGHT TURN

Signaling

Of the many American peculiarities described in this booklet, this one definitively deserves a special mention. While the motor vehicle codes around the world are comparable, this practice stands out.

Before being allowed to take the practical driving test, to actually drive off the Department of Motor Vehicle (DMV) parking lot, student drivers will be asked by the driving test inspector to lower the driver's side window and demonstrate the hand signals for turning left, for turning right, and for stopping. (Only few other mostly English-speaking countries also require drivers to know some hand signals.)

A word of warning, the inspectors take this test very seriously and if you don't execute properly you might not even get to start your car's motor!

For the motorcycle license test, you also will have to demonstrate the proper hand signals, before being asked to prove your driving skills.

Unbelievable but true: In many states you can a get your motorcycle license without ever leaving the DMV parking lot! In those states you simply will be required to drive several circles and figure-eight patterns without your feet ever touching the ground.

It actually makes a lot of sense for bicyclists and even motorcyclists to know hand signals. But for car drivers?

It looks like the lawmakers are not putting a whole lot of trust in todays' technology, and this at a time when driverless cars are being tested on the roads. Go figure.

Vehicle Code

Many new U.S. residents are surprised to learn that their national driving license does not qualify them automatically for a U.S. license. On the contrary, many states require both a written and a driving test, citing the obvious fact that driving laws differ among countries.

In fact, vehicle codes also vary among U.S. states. For example, in some states, drivers must "curb" their wheels when parking on a hill. This involves turning the wheels to the left after parking uphill (or to the right when parking downhill) and letting the tires slip up against the curb so they are blocked from rolling.

Be forewarned that where this rule exists, it is strictly enforced, and this ticket can be costly.

Overall, U.S. drivers tend to comply with the motor vehicle code, with one major exception: Far too many actively disregard the law about using the left-hand lane on the highway only for passing.

Instead, motorists will drive continuously in the left-hand lane, pushing others to pass on the right. Even when the highway is nearly empty, some drivers will not only stay put in the left-hand lane but also feel comfortable driving below normal traffic speed.

Although the speed limit in the United States is lower than for in countries like Germany, it is quite unnerving for foreigners to have to watch for cars passing on the left and on the right.

Way of Life

Air Conditioning

Air conditioning is a way of life in North America. Nearly every public building is equipped with air conditioning, and the U.S. Department of Energy website says at least three-quarters of private residents also have A/C units in their home. Even in places like Seattle, where air conditioning was once uncommon, people now have cooling units installed, not least because of climate change and other weather extremes.

Americans expect air conditioning wherever they go (e.g. work, restaurants, movie theaters, and at home), and they don't seem to mind the cost of running these units. For instance, little consideration is given to the impact on the ecosystem as the A/C system runs full blast even when windows and doors are wide open. Some keep their A/C running even when the outside temperature is mild, say around 20°C (68°F), and there no need for air conditioning.

Public places are some of the biggest offenders. Supermarkets often set their temperatures at the unnecessarily chilly levels of 12-15°C (54-59°F) or lower. Movie theaters and restaurants are also notorious for blasting the A/C at very low temperatures.

Americans may be used to near arctic conditions being recreated indoors, but people from other cultures generally find the temperature in public places way too low for their comfort.

The foreigners are easy to spot: They are the ones putting on a sweater or jacket before entering any public building.

Banking

U.S. banking processes can be rather baffling to a foreigner. On one hand there is the convenience of countless Automated Teller Machines (ATMs) and being able to get cash-back at grocery stores. On the other hand, many banking processes seem more complicated than necessary.

Question: Why are personal checks still so widely used when bank transfers are so easy to do? Not only does the check printing create additional cost, but it generates extra work for both the customer and the bank. On top of it, regular checks drawn on a personal checking account are not even always accepted. When they are, the credit to the account can be held by the bank for as long as 10 days. (Banks argue that they must wait for the money to be transferred into the account.)

By the way, a good many employees are still paid weekly by check. Why is such a slow process still used when there are better alternatives? By the way, it is estimated that nearly 8% of Americans don't have a bank account.

Of course, once you learn the exorbitant price of most wire transfers, you will happily revert to sending a personal check by postal service. Or you simply sign-up for one of the newer internet banking institutions, which now offer borderless accounts with easy in-app money transfer and currency exchange options.

Need foreign cash for your travel? Not many banks offer that service any longer and, even if they do, you might have to wait a couple of days before receiving the new currency notes. So, don't wait till the last minute.

Cost of Living

Where you are relocating from will largely determine how you appraise the cost of living in the United States. While some things may seem excessively costly, others might strike you as incredibly inexpensive.

More than anything, the advertised and marked prices will feel confusing.

For starters, you cannot rely on the advertised prices to be equal to the actual amount of your purchase, as taxes will be added at checkout. In most states, only professional services—legal, accounting, consulting, engineering, training, design services, and so forth—tend to be tax-exempt.

And it does not end there. On top of the tax amount, you must add a tip to the advertised price. Don't think for one minute that tipping in these situations is optional.

Tips are the norm in restaurants (as discussed earlier), but that is far from the only place they are expected. Hairdressers, luggage handlers, cab drivers, hotel valets and housekeepers, and so many others—even people who push the wheelchairs in the airport—all rely on tips.

This general dependence on customers tipping surely has to do with the low wages most these professions pay. Still, it makes it difficult to figure the final price in advance.

Unfortunately, to some foreigners this is reminiscent of countries where you are expected to grease the wheels to get things done.

Health Care | Services

We all have heard about the exorbitant costs of medical procedures, the scandals around drug pricing, and the high monthly premiums for health insurance in the United States, one of the most expensive health care systems in the world.

What might be surprising to newcomers is how U.S. health providers interact with their patients. Here a few examples:

- A nurse or someone on the doctor's staff will call you a day before to remind you of your appointment.

- On the day of the doctor's visit (and before you see any medical personnel), you first must pay your out-of-pocket fee. At that time, you also might be given a "hospital bracelet" to uniquely identify you to the doctor.

- Once the nurse calls your name, no matter what the reason for your office visit, you will be weighed, and your temperature and blood pressure will be checked.

- If your provider is a major health clinic, your blood might be drawn by a nurse working in an assembly line-type setting!

All this in the name of efficiency and best practice. By the time you get to talk to a doctor about the reason for your visit, you will already feel thoroughly identified and assessed.

You might also be a bit concerned about all that data being collected when you simply wanted to talk about how to prevent sickness while traveling.

Health Care | Prescriptions

The influence of the Puritan settlers can still be felt in this land of excess. This ambivalence becomes clear when, for example, taking a closer look at how alcohol and prescription drugs are advertised and dispensed.

The assortment of alcohol in stores is broad and one can even buy it 24/7 in many states. The flip side is the restrictions around alcohol use. The legal drinking age in most states is 21, higher than other countries around the world. And it is illegal to carry open containers in public.

The circumvention of this is another Americanism: People will "disguise" their beverages by slipping them into tall brown bags. The irony is that people only drink from tall brown bags when they are drinking alcoholic beverages.

The American ambiguity is also evident when looking at the number of advertisements for prescription drugs, which are prolific, and the standard for dispensing the medicine, which is stringent.

Many heavy-duty drugs are advertised without restriction on TV with slogans like: "Ask your doctor about X." Once your doctor gives you a prescription for X, however, the pharmacist will count the exact number of pills ordered before dispensing them in a generic orange plastic container with a child-safety cap. No handing out of a standardized package of pills here.

Sadly, as the current U.S. opioid epidemic shows, once you have a prescription, it is not hard to get it renewed. This effectively defeats the purpose of counting the pills...

Lawyers

If the latest numbers from the American Bar Association are to be believed, there is one active lawyer for every 245 people in the United States. That gives the country one of the world's top per-capita proportion of lawyers.

The number of lawyers also underscores how litigious the country is. Disagreements are quickly seen as legal puzzles to be resolved in court.

As in other cultures, the language of legal documents is pretty much illegible unless you have some legal experience of your own. For that reason, legal advice is recommended for almost any contract you consider signing, even if lawyer's fees are notoriously steep. (And they are, easily ranging between $100 and $500 per hour.)

Too often foreigners find their hyphenated or multipart family name to be their first legal hurdle. Any misspelling, or even an additional space between names on any kind of official document, can later lead to problems. So be sure to double check any legal paper before you sign it. Otherwise you might later have to prove that the clerk made a mistake and you never had any intention of making a name change. And good luck with that.

A word of advice, should you find yourself in any kind of legal misunderstanding or dispute: Don't ever hesitate to get a lawyer. In the end, it probably will not only be the best, but overall also the most economical solution to your legal issues.

The Foreigners' Perspective

Office Work

Depending on your own cultural background, the American work setting can be quite surprising.

- As previously mentioned, the air-conditioning leaves many foreigners struggling to stay warm and wondering if the low temperature might be a ploy to keep them alert.

- Even though brown-bag lunches have become more common around the world, the American version can make people from other cultures feel awkward. Foreigners do expect work luncheons to be more of a social (and culinary) event meant to strengthen relationships.

- One can debate the merits of open workspaces and cubicles, but there's no arguing that they are now a reality in many places. At a time when over 60 percent of the population is overweight, some cubicles in America seem particularly small.

- As personal workspaces get smaller and smaller, lobbies are getting bigger and grander. It probably comes down to the idea that one never gets a second chance to make a first impression.

- Employee of the Month is a popular recognition in America and the awards will often be showcased in a company's spacious lobby. Unfortunately, it is not always clear how the honored employee actually benefits from the award.

Those peculiarities aside, the remarkable thing about the U.S. workplace is that you might get hired for a particular job at a junior pay grade then find yourself promoted within a few months to a senior position with a considerably higher pay. Now that is motivating!

Patriotism

Every country in the world fosters patriotic feelings and pride in its cultural achievements, as well they should. Over centuries, each country has developed its own norms, rituals, and customs, some more unusual than others.

One U.S. custom that surprises most foreigners is the importance and omnipresence of the U.S flag. The flying of the American flag outside every government building and post office is indeed a very visible patriotic manifestation, only topped by the flags also being displayed inside many buildings, notably in every courtroom across the nation as well as in schoolrooms. Some schools even have monthly flag ceremonies.

Foreigners are generally not used to such a ubiquitous display of a national flag and wonder why so many are needed. Or as one expat asked, "Are Americans afraid they'll somehow forget in which country they live?"

Another notable expression of patriotism is the high profile of the Pledge of Allegiance. Even at professional events that don't require attendants to be American citizens, recitation of the pledge often is part of the agenda. Realtor meetings are one example.

These moments can be extremely awkward for foreigners. What are they expected to do when everyone else stands with their hand across their hearts to say the pledge?

It is intriguing to see the importance given to public displays of patriotism and how much they are part of the fabric of everyday life.

Pets

There is no doubt about it, Americans love their pets.

This country has the highest number of cats (86 million) and dogs (78 million) worldwide. On average, every other resident has a cat or a dog. Yet it is not the ubiquity but the pet owners' behaviors toward their pets that leave expats shaking their heads.

For instance, while it might be rewarding for pet owners to put their mascots in silly dresses and organize birthday parties for them, it is doubtful it meets the pets' needs. And what about a dog perched on its owner's lap, paws resting on the open car windowsill, ears flapping in the wind? Americans consider this extremely cute. In a way, it is.

But is it safe for the dog and the driver? An accident involving a van whose driver was distracted by an unrestrained dog caused writer Stephen King, walking along the side of the road, years of pain.

Of course, they are in no way the only culture humanizing pets, even sometimes spoiling the animals with treats to the point of making them sick. Nevertheless, Americans have definitely developed a peculiar attitude about pets.

What does seem peculiar in the United States is how dogs are treated like children, even sharing the bed with them. At the same time they are not allowed in restaurants for hygienic reasons.

Question: How can it then be hygienic to share a bed with your pet?

The Foreigners' Perspective

Public Bathrooms

Once again, we have to mention bathrooms, as they are a fundamental and essential element of daily life at home as well as on the road.

There are lots of good things to be said about public bathrooms in America.

- First and foremost, they are usually very clean.

- They are almost always equipped with generous amounts of toilet paper, which is not necessarily the case in other countries.

- They are free. There is generally no charge for access like in some countries, where without the exact change you are doomed.

- Another outstanding service are the toilet seat covers. Of course, one can argue over their usefulness in effectively preventing the spread of germs and bacteria, but once accustomed to them, you will forever miss them on your trips abroad. (You can always buy travel packages available online).

It is an open secret that U.S. culture is still rather puritanical and prudish. As mentioned before, that is surely one of the major reasons that most homes offer the luxury of one bathroom for almost every bedroom.

With that in mind, it seems particularly odd that public bathroom stalls are not very private at all. Rarely do their walls and doors reach all the way to the floor or the ceiling. And the gap between the door and the stall frame is often so big that anyone can catch a glimpse of the individual sitting on the throne.

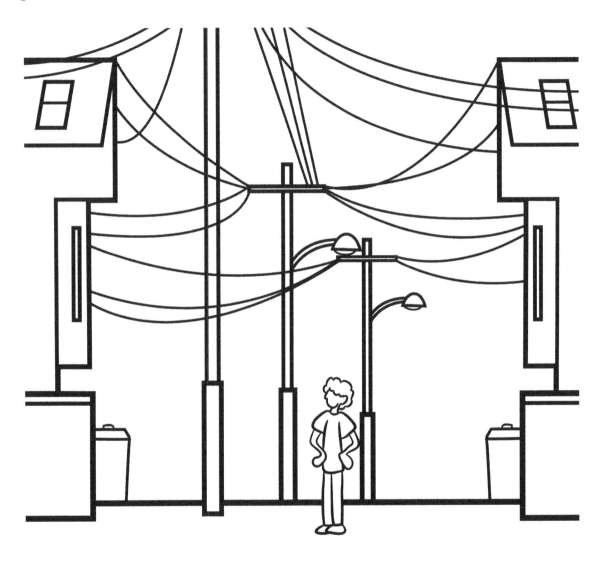

The Foreigners' Perspective

Public Infrastructure

Skeins of electrical lines still hang over many U.S. neighborhoods even though the consensus is that power lines should be subterranean.

Since burying the lines underground is very expensive, streets crisscrossed by overhead electrical lines will definitively be with us for a while longer. As long as that is the case, public and private grid providers will continue to share the same poles. But they won't share the management of their lines. Therein lies one major challenge for infrastructure planning and upgrades.

Another throwback in the public service arena comes in the form of huge, endearingly old-fashioned-looking fire engines. In many countries, trucks of that size would never be able to navigate the historically narrow, winding streets.

And that brings us to public transportation or, rather, the lack of it outside big cities. In a country so big and with so many sparsely populated areas, it would be asking too much to expect public transportation to reach every hammock. Still, existing public transit has been woefully neglected over the decades.

Only lately are Americans (re)discovering the convenience of shared transportation services like Lime, Uber, Lyft and, to a lesser degree, the benefits of true public transportation like buses and trains.

Other public infrastructures, including highways and streets, also have been denied the attention they need. The potholes everywhere are a reminder of a German saying: "One hole next to another—and still somehow it all holds together."

Schooling

This topic alone could fill a book on its own, but there are a few standout items that foreigners should know:

- Few children go to school on their own by bike or on foot. Most take a school bus or are driven. This causes daily traffic jams at the schools.

- In primary school, there is a focus on spelling and communication that is unmatched in most other cultures.

- Any effort by the students is highly praised and there are awards given for many kinds of achievements.

- Teachers stay in their own classrooms while the students move from room to room. High school students can largely select their study subjects. Therefore, they find themselves with different students in each class.

- The U.S. flag is displayed in classrooms and the Pledge of Allegiance is recited daily.

- School budgets are set by multiplying a per-student dollar amount (which varies widely) by the number of children and youth enrolled at a school. The students and the funds that correspond to them may be transferred from public schools to private charter schools. These institutions are profit-oriented and have few restrictions in terms of curriculum and teacher certification.

Kids transferring from a school abroad are amazed by the range of classes and school activities, including choir, theater, and sports. Once they conquer the language barrier, students generally enjoy going to school here, and many achieve even better test scores in the United States than they had back home.

The Foreigners' Perspective

Shopping & Service

The United States is the land of 24/7 shopping and huge malls. But a shift is underway.

Today big shopping malls are springing up on other continents while U.S. malls are rapidly losing clients to the convenience of online shopping. Still, you should visit at least a few malls as their parking lots alone are impressive.

Be aware that American shopping malls are not just for shopping. They are the modern-day equivalent of a village promenade, where young and old go to see and be seen. In colder regions they even double as gyms in the winter as seniors meet to exercise and walk in a warm, dry setting.

No matter where you're headed in the mall, you will find service personnel welcoming you with a smile, a shopping experience that differs markedly from that of Europe and other places where monosyllabic answers and a sour face are unfortunately too often the norm.

U.S. salespeople introduce themselves by name and make small talk not necessarily connected to the task at hand. This kindly service with a smile is not merely the result of good sales training. It is part of the larger American easy-going hospitality culture. Even if the service is not always competent, it is always friendly.

Now before you overcharge your credit card, remember that just like restaurants, the advertised price is not the final one. Sales tax still is added at checkout.

Sporting Events

Sporting events and the dedicated sports channels on TV are big business in America. And the players and teams are frequently hailed as today's heroes.

The Super Bowl, the annual American football championship, is the most-watched U.S. sporting event every year. In 2018, more than 100 million people watched two U.S. teams compete for the title.

Another main annual sporting event is Major League Baseball's televised World Series, a playoff that, despite its name, only features teams from the United States and Canada.

From the Foreigners' Perspective, these sports seem slow moving with lengthy breaks to review strategies, many confusing rules, and no opportunity to root and cheer for one's own national team. The actual spectators of these events, meanwhile, often seem more interested in the tailgate parties, the foods available, or the advertisements aired during the games.

It is also surprising that in a country built on equality for all, men's baseball is big business, but women's softball games are hardly televised (and relatively few men play this sport).

One thing all U.S. sporting events do have in common is a deafening noise level created by shouting players, musical interludes, the fervent cheering of the fans and, of course, the cheerleaders.

There is one question pretty much all foreigners have: Why have Americans only in recent years started to develop a passion for soccer, the most popular sport anywhere else in the world?

Get in Touch

Connect with us on

www.ForeignersPerspective.com

And tell us about your cultural adventures, mishaps
or funny experiences...

We would love to hear from you!

32213477R00077

Made in the USA
Middletown, DE
08 January 2019